Let's Explore KANJI

A Picture Tour of Japanese Characters

はじめてのかんじ

Bret Mayer ブレット・メイヤー

Jリサーチ出版

Preface

Welcome to 『Let's Explore KANJI』 an introduction to written characters used to express Japanese words. In Japan, there are currently 2,136 so-called "general use" kanji, which are commonly used in print, television and on signage. This book introduces about 100 characters learned during the 1st and 2nd years of elementary schools in Japan. So, once you finish, you'll have the awesome reading comprehension of an 8-year old. But, don't despair! Each page includes phrases containing several vocabulary words using that page's kanji along with a variety of other kanji sprinkled in for bonus learning opportunities!

Some tips for getting the most out of this book:

✔ **Practice writing each kanji following the stroke order provided.**

Stroke order is important because it builds muscle memory. Stroke order gives you a guide to follow every time you write, and once your hand gets used to that rhythm, writing will be like second nature!

✔ **Take note of the readings that represent the sound and meaning of the kanji.**

Incorporate these into your writing practice. For example, don't just write 火…火…火… over and over, write 火 カ ひ fire … 火 カ ひ fire… On'yomi in katakana, kun'yomi in hiragana (you'll learn about these in just a bit), and then…

2

✔ Color-code kanji vs readings vs English.

火 カ ひ fire⋯ 火 カ ひ fire⋯

This creates vibrant notes that are easy to review and adds a little fun to the repetitive task of writing. Feel free to remix this to fit your specific study style⋯ change the colors, use pens or pencils, write out the provided vocabulary, etc. Flash cards are great, too, but are mostly visual. If you review readings and English with flash cards, be sure to at least practice writing the kanji itself regularly.

✔ Once you've mastered the featured 100 kanji⋯

Go back and read through the included phrases. Each one contains several vocabulary words using that page's kanji along with many other kanji and compounds. Compare the English and Japanese to pick up even more kanji and analyze how different ideas are expressed in Japanese. Practice writing new kanji you come across and see if you recognize any new patterns. Get creative and try swapping out some words to make your own phrases!

✔ ⋯And don't forget the lists in the back!

Included in Chapter 2 are several lists with useful or interesting kanji and vocabulary words. Some of them (months of the year, numbers) are crucial for the Japanese learner, while others are just for fun! Being able to smoothly write out some of the more difficult kanji featured there is quite impressive to the average Japanese person and can be a great icebreaker!

Bret Mayer

はじめに

日本語の書き文字の超入門書である『Let's Explore KANJI』の世界へようこそ。日本では、現在2,136語のいわゆる常用漢字があり、印刷物やテレビ、看板などに使われているよ。この本では、主に小学校1,2年で習う約100語の漢字を取り上げているよ。だから、あなたがこの本を読み終わったときには、8才くらいの漢字力が身についたことになるね。でも絶望しちゃだめだよ！それぞれのページに掲載されているフレーズは、取り上げた漢字以外にもさまざまな漢字を使っていて、さらなる勉強の機会を提供しているんだ！

この本を最大限に活用するためのアドバイス：

✔ **それぞれの漢字は、書き順に従って書く練習をすること。**
書き順は重要なんだ。なぜなら手の動きが漢字を記憶するからだよ。書き順は、あなたが漢字を書くときには毎回道しるべとなるよ。そしてあなたが一度書き順のリズムを覚えたら、書くことは習性となって身についているはずだよ！

✔ **漢字の音と意味を表す読みかたは、ノートに書いて覚えること。**
これらは書くことの練習に組み込もう。例えば、火、火、火…と何度も漢字だけ書いて覚えるよりも、火、カ、ひ、fire…、火、カ、ひ、fire…火、カ、ひ、fire…と音読みはカタカナで訓読みはひらがなで書くとわかりやすいよ。（この本では音読みと訓読みは少しだけ勉強するよ）そして…

4

✔ 色で区別する　＜漢字 vs 読み vs 英語＞

火、カ、ひ、fire…火、カ、ひ、fire…

上記のような鮮やかなノートは、復習しやすいし、同じ文字をくり返し書く退屈な作業を少し楽しくしてくれるよ。色を変えたり、鉛筆を使ったり、本の中にある語彙を書き出したり、あなたの学習スタイルにあうように自由に変えてみてね。
フラッシュカードを使うのもとても効果的だよ、ただしとても視覚的だね。もしあなたが読みかたと英語をフラッシュカードで復習するときは、漢字の書き取りの練習も定期的にやることをオススメするよ。

✔ あなたがこの本の 100 語をマスターしたら…

もう一度はじめに戻り、フレーズを読んでみよう。それぞれのフレーズには、取り上げた漢字以外の重要な漢字も含まれているよ。英語と日本語を比べながら、たくさんの漢字を覚えて日本語の表現のしかたを分析してみよう。そしてあなたがはじめて出会った新しい漢字の書き取り練習をして、新しいパターンを見つけてみよう。さらに、いくつかの言葉を入れ替えて、あなたのオリジナルのフレーズを作ってみよう！

✔ そして、2 章の漢字リストも忘れずに！

2章の種類別の一覧表は、身近で便利な漢字やおもしろい漢字を集めたよ。いくつかの漢字（月や数）は、日本語学習者にとってとても重要な一方、ほかのものは単純におもしろいよ！ここで取り上げたような難しい漢字がスラスラ書けると、たいていの日本人にとってとても印象的だし、ステキなアイスブレーカーになれるよ！

ブレット・メイヤー

Contents

Chapter 1
Basic kanji　基本の漢字

もくじ

Chapter 2
List of kanji by concept
種類別の漢字一覧表

How to use this book

Chapter 1
Basic kanji　基本の漢字

100 kanji ordered by Japanese syllabary.
漢字は音読みのア行から五十音順に並んでいるよ。

The stroke order is given as a guide.
書き順はガイドとして役立ててね。

1 : On' yomi（音読み）

2 : Kun'yomi（訓読み）

◀€ : Pronunciation（発音）

EN : Meaning（英語の意味）

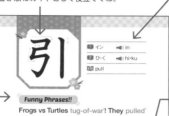

1 イン　　◀€ in

2 ひ・く　◀€ hi·ku

EN pull

Funny Phrases!!

Frogs vs Turtles tug-of-war! They pulled²
with all their might, but... it ended in a
tie³.

カエル対カメの綱引き！一生懸命引いた²が…引き分け³に終わった。

Writing Styles　引　引　引

🐱 ネコはかせの まめちしき

引 is used to label door handles as PULL. 押 is
PUSH.

「引」は、よくドアに書かれている。「引」は引く、「押」は押すという意味。

18

Writing Styles show
alternate ways of drawing
each character commonly
used in calligraphy.
Simplification of kanji
through brush calligraphy
was instrumental in creating
hiragana!

ライティングスタイルは、書道で
よく使われる漢字のスタイルだよ。
毛筆を通した漢字の単純化は、
ひらがなを作る助けになったん
だ。草書→行書→楷書の順に
並んでいるよ。

There are many opinions
regarding writing styles, so
consider this a
representative example.

ライティングスタイルには諸説
あるけど、代表的なものを載せ
ているよ。

Professor Neko teaches
you interesting trivia about
Japanese language and
culture!
ネコはかせは、まめちしきを教
えてくれるよ。

Bret-sensei explains the
idea behind the character's
original design!
ぶㇾせんせいは、漢字の成り立ち
を紹介するよ。

Wacky phrases in Japanese and English
using featured kanji. There are just silly
phrases to show words in the context of a
sentence. Don't take them too seriously.
取り上げた漢字を使ったおもしろいフレーズだよ！
ジョークだから、内容は信じちゃダメよ。

本書の使いかた

Chapter 2
List of kanji by concept 種類別の漢字一覧表

🗨 : Kun' yomi（訓読み）
🔊 : Pronunciation（発音）
EN : Meaning（英語の意味）

Body 体

頭	🗨 あたま 🔊 : atama EN head 👅 頭上注意　Watch your head!
目	🗨 め 🔊 : me EN eye 👅 目蓋　eyelid
髪	🗨 かみ 🔊 : kami EN hair 👅 散髪　haircut
鼻	🗨 はな 🔊 : hana EN nose 👅 鼻をかむ　to blow your nose
口	🗨 くち 🔊 : kuchi EN mouth 👅 口笛　whistle
耳	🗨 みみ 🔊 : mimi EN ear 👅 耳たぶ　earlobe
首	🗨 くび 🔊 : kubi EN neck 👅 首輪　collar, necklace

121

Lists of kanji found in various aspects of daily life. Picture are included to help you learn!

日常生活で使われる漢字を9つの分野に分けて一覧表にしたよ。新しい漢字を覚えるにはイラストが役に立つはずだよ！

9

How to download audio files

STEP1

Visit https://audiobook.jp/exchange/jresearch

※ Enter the above URL into your preferred browser or visit the publisher's official site (http://www.jresearch.co.jp) and click the banner labelled 「音声ダウンロード」.

STEP2

Complete registration for a free membership at audiobook.jp.

※ Download of the audio files requires completion of (free!) member registration at audiobook.jp. Click 「無料会員登録」 to begin. Enter your name 「名前」, email 「メールアドレス」 and desired password 「パスワード」.

STEP3

After registration, return to https://audiobook.jp/exchange/jresearch . Enter your serial number 「24499」 in the input box labeled 「シリアルコード入力欄」 and click the turquoise button labeled 「送信する」 below.

※ The files will now be added to your Library 「ライブラリ」.

STEP4

Download your desired audio files!

※ If using a smartphone, instruction will appear for downloading the 「audiobook.jp」app. You can also find the app by searching "otobank inc." or 「オーディオブック」 in the iOS or Android app store.

※ If using a PC, click 「ライブラリ」 from the left-side menu and select your desired files.

NOTE

- You can play the audio files on PC or iPhone/Android smartphones and tablets.
- There is no limit to how many times you can download and play the files.
- For help regarding download of the audio files, please e-mail info@febe.jp （weekdays between 10AM-8PM）

音声ダウンロードのしかた

STEP1

インターネットで https://audiobook.jp/exchange/jresearch
にアクセス!

※上記 URL を入力いただくか、J リサーチ出版のサイトの「音声ダウンロード」
　バナーをクリックしてください。

STEP2

表示されたページから、audiobook.jp の会員登録ページへ。

※音声のダウンロードには、オーディオブック配信サービス audiobook.jp への
　会員登録（無料）が必要です。

STEP3

登録後、再度 STEP1 のサイトに再アクセスし、シリアルコード
「24499」を入力後、[送信]をクリック!

※作品がライブラリに追加されたと案内が出ます。

STEP4

必要な音声ファイルをダウンロード!

※スマートフォンの場合は、アプリ「audiobook.jp」の案内が出ますので、ア
　プリからご利用ください。
※ PC の場合は、「ライブラリ」から音声ファイルをダウンロードしてご利用くだ
　さい。

ご注意

● PC からでも、iPhone や Android のスマートフォンやタブレットからでも
　音声を再生いただけます。
● 音声は何度でもダウンロード・再生いただくことができます。
● ダウンロードについてのお問い合わせ先：info@febe.jp（受付時間：平日
　10 ～ 20 時）

What are kanji?
漢字ってなんだろう？

There are three different kinds of characters in the Japanese language; hiragana, katakana and kanji.

日本語には、3種類の文字があるよ。それぞれひらがな、カタカナ、漢字と呼ばれているんだ。

 ## The History of kanji　漢字の歴史

Kanji were developed in China over 3000 years ago. They began as crude pictures to represent spoken words in the Chinese language. Over time, characters were combined and expanded to express more complex ideas while efforts to unify and streamline their writing have brought us to the kanji we common use today.

漢字は今から3000年以上前に中国で生まれたんだ。彼らは話している言葉を大雑把な絵にして表し始めたんだ。長い年月をかけて、文字は、結びついたり広く展開したりして、より複雑な表現ができるようになる一方、簡易化したり統一化したりして、今日わたしたちが使っている漢字になったんだ。

Reading kanji　漢字の読みかた

Most kanji have two types of readings: on' yomi（音読み）and kun' yomi（訓読み）. On' yomi = SOUND—the original Chinese pronunciation adapted into the Japanese language. Kun'yomi = MEANING—i.e., a Japanese word assigned to that character. For 山, サン is the SOUND and やま (mountain) the MEANING. Be aware each kanji can have multiple SOUNDS and MEANINGS, though usually its MEANINGS are closely related.

ほとんどの漢字は、2種類の読みかたがあるよ。音読みと訓読みだ。音読みは、もともとの中国の読みかたが、日本語になったものだ。一方、訓読みは意味を表すよ。つまり漢字に日本語の意味を与えたんだ。例えば「山」という漢字は「サン」が音読みで、「やま」が意味（訓読み）だね。たいていの漢字は、それぞれ関連はあるけれど、何通りもの読みかたがあるから注意が必要だよ。

 ## Radical　部首

> Some kanji come from simple pictures…
> いくつかの漢字は、単純にそのものの形を表しているよ。

犬　dog　いぬ

象　elephant　ぞう

鳥　bird　とり

But these are very few in number…
でもこのような漢字はとても少ないんだ…

Most kanji combine multiple pictures to form complex meanings··· but there are helpful patterns!
Some parts give you a hint as to the meaning:

多くの漢字は、複雑な意味を表すために複数のパーツを組み合わせて作られているよ…でもそれらには、覚えるのに役立つパターンがあるんだ:

 さんずい　water ·······························

汽	海	池	湖	泳	深
steam	ocean	pond	lake	swim	deep

 Why does the 漢 in 漢字 have water?
なぜ「漢字」の「漢」にも「さんずい」が使われているの?

漢 refers to the Han River in China, and subsequently the Han Dynasty of 200 BC – 200 AD and Han Chinese ethnic group.
漢字 are literally the characters 字 of the Han 漢 people.

漢とは、もともと中国の川を表していたんだ。続いて紀元前200年～200年頃に中国全土を支配した王朝を漢王朝と呼び、その主要な民族を漢民族と言うようになったんだ。漢字は、漢民族の文字という意味だよ。

 しめすへん　ritual ·······································

祝	神	祈	礼	福
celebrate	deity	prayer	etiquette	blessing

Holidays in Japan are called 祝日, using the kanji for celebration and day.

日本では、国で定めた祝いの日は「祝日」と呼ばれているよ。

14

てへん　**hand** ························

拾	捨	打	投	折	握
pick up	toss out	strike	throw	fold/break	grasp

Origami 折り紙 uses the kanji for fold and paper.

紙を（手で）折るから、「折り紙」と言うよ。

握手 is a handshake, while 握り寿司 is sushi rice rolled in the hand with fish placed on top.

（手を）握るから「握手」、（手で）米を丸めて、魚を上に乗せるから「握り寿司」と言うよ。

> Some parts give a hint as to the reading!
> いくつかのパーツは、読むためのヒントになるよ!

Kanji with 且 are often ソ
且を含む漢字は、よく「ソ」と読むよ。

狙撃手 sniper	祖先、先祖 ancestors
粗末 rough, coarse	組織 organization
租税 tax	阻止 obstruction

…but not always!
…ただし、必ずというわけではないんだ!

査定 assessment	助言 advice

15

Kanji with 召 are often ショウ
召を含む漢字は、よく「ショウ」と読むよ。

召喚 <ruby>しょうかん</ruby> summon

招待 <ruby>しょうたい</ruby> invitation

照明 <ruby>しょうめい</ruby> (electric) lighting

昭和 <ruby>しょうわ</ruby> Showa (era)

自己紹介 <ruby>じこしょうかい</ruby> self-introduction

詔勅 <ruby>しょうちょく</ruby> imperial edict

…but not always!
…ただし、必ずというわけではないんだ!

超能力 <ruby>ちょうのうりょく</ruby> supernatural ability

To some extent, kanji have a logical pattern to them, but these characters have evolved and changed over thousands of years, so it's not always perfect… BUT recognizing these patterns and hints when they appear can help immensely with high-level kanji study! For now, let's take a look at 100 basic kanji as taught in Japan during 1st and 2nd year of elementary school. Your kanji journey begins on the next page!

ある程度、これらのパターンは論理的に説明できるよ。でも漢字は何千年もかけて進化しているものだから、いつも完璧というわけではないんだ。でも意味を理解したり、読んだりするときに、どの部分がヒントになるかを知っておくと、ハイレベルの漢字の勉強にとても役立つよ! さあ!日本の小学校で漢字を教わっているように、100の基本の漢字を見ていこう!次のページからあなたの漢字の旅が始まるよ!

Chapter 1

Basic kanji 100

基本の漢字
100

1	イン	🔊 in
2	ひ・く	🔊 hi・ku
EN	pull	

Funny Phrases!!

Frogs vs Turtles tug-of-war[1]! They pulled[2] with all their might, but... it ended in a draw[3].

カエル対カメの綱引き[1]！　一生懸命引いた[2] が…引き分け[3] に終わった。

| Writing Styles | 引 | 引 | 引 |

ネコはかせの まめちしき

引 is used to label door handles as PULL. 押 is PUSH.

「引」は、よくドアに書かれているよ。「引」は引く、「押」は押すという意味。

1 ウ	🔊 u
2 みぎ	🔊 migi
EN right	

Funny Phrases!!

We're going right¹, so signal a right turn²
with your right hand³.

右¹に行くので、右手³で右折²することを合図して。

| **Writing Styles** | 右 | 右 | 右 |

ぶせんせいの
ちょっとひとこと

A right hand 𠂇 holding on
object 口.

右手でものを持っている様子を表しているよ。

19

1 ウ 🔊 u

2 あめ 🔊 ame

EN rain

Funny Phrases!!

Tomorrow's baseball game will be canceled in the event of rain[1], but the horse race is on rain or shine[2]. Whether it rains[3] or not, tomorrow's gonna be a fun day!

あしたの野球の試合は雨天中止[1]ですが、競馬は雨天決行[2]。雨[3]が降っても降らなくても、楽しい1日になりそう！

| Writing Styles | | | |

 ネコはかせの まめちしき

Rain 雨, rain is found in many weather-related kanji, such as cloud 雲 and snow 雪.

雨という漢字は、雲や雪のように、部首として天気に関係するいろいろな漢字に使われているよ。

1 エン ◀ en

2 まる・い ◀ maru・i

EN Yen, circle

Funny Phrases!!

The secret to a harmonious marriage[1]?
That's easy. When your wife gets angry,
give her 10,000 yen[2].

夫婦円満[1]の秘訣とは？それは簡単
さ。奥さんが不機嫌になったとき、
1万円[2]をあげるのだ。

| Writing Styles | | | |

 ネコはかせのまめちしき

You may sometimes see 圓 in place of 円 to
mean Japanese yen. 圓 is the older form of this
kanji.

日本円を表すときに「円」の代わりに「圓」が使われることがあるよ。「圓」
は「円」の古い形なんだ。

| 1 | エン | 🔊 en |
| 2 | その | 🔊 sono |

EN garden, park

Funny Phrases!!

A fun day for the kids at preschool[1]!
They went to play at the zoo[2] and the
amusement park[3].

幼稚園 の子どもたちの楽しい1
日！動物園 と遊園地 に遊びに
行った。

| **Writing Styles** | 園 | 園 | 園 |

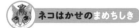 ネコはかせの**まめちしき**

園 is a deliberately designed and constructed
garden, while 苑 is a more free and naturally
growing garden.

「園」は計画的に作られた庭園、「苑」はより自然にできた庭園というイメージ
だよ。

1	エン	🔊 en
2	とお・い	🔊 tō・i
EN	far, distant

Funny Phrases!!

They said we'd go far[1] for our school trip[2], but to think we'd go to the moon!

遠足₂で遠い₁ところに行くと言ったが、まさか月までとは！

| Writing Styles | | | |

 ネコはかせのまめちしき

Notice how 園 and 遠 both contain 袁 and share a reading of エン. It's not a coincidence! Recognizing these hints within kanji can really help with kanji study!

「園」と「遠」はどちらも〈袁〉が含まれていて、「エン」という読み方も一緒だね。このようなヒントを理解しておくと、漢字の勉強の助けになるよ！

1	オン	🔊 on
2	おと	🔊 oto
EN	sound, tone	

Funny Phrases!!

I wish the remote's mute[1] button could turn off not just sound[2] from the TV or music[3] from the radio, but the volume[4] of your voice as well...

リモコンの消音[1] ボタンはテレビの
音[2] やラジオの音楽[3] だけではなく、
あなたの声の音量[4] も消せればいい
のにな…

| **Writing Styles** | 音 | 音 | 音 |

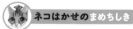 ネコはかせの まめちしき

音 (sound) + 色 (color) means "tone" 音色.

「音色」は、「音」+「色」で、それぞれの音の感覚的な特性という意味だよ。

1	カ	ka
2	した、 さが・る	shita, saga・ru
EN	down, below, under	

Funny Phrases!!

I bow my head[1] before your adept chopstick usage. I'm very unskilled[2].

あなたのお箸の使いっぷりに頭が下がります。わたしはとても下手です。
※「下手」は特別な読み方です。

| **Writing
Styles** | 下 | 下 | 下 |

 ネコはかせのまめちしき

…に頭が下がります means you are in awe or feel great respect towards another for their efforts or achievement.

「…に頭が下がります」は、ほかの人の努力や成果に敬意を表すときに使うよ。

1	カ	🔈 ka
2	ひ	🔈 hi
EN	fire	

Funny Phrases!!

"Let's go see a volcano[1] on Tuesday[2]!" suggested my Martian[3] friend.

「火曜日 は火山 を見に行こう！」と火星人 の友だちが提案した。

Writing Styles	

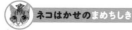 ネコはかせのまめちしき

火 is used to refer to the planet Mars (火星) and the day Tuesday (火曜日).

「火」は、「火星」や「火曜日」を表すときに使われるんだ。

1	カ	🔊 ka
2	はな	🔊 hana
EN	flower	

Funny Phrases!!

Uh oh! The cops are here! Quick, take the flowers¹ out of that vase² and hide the fireworks³ in there!

ヤバい！サツが来た！早く花びん²から花¹を出して花火³を隠して！

| Writing Styles | も | 花 | 花 |

ぶせんせいのちょっとひとこと

Simplified from 華, which was designed after the shape of a flower.

「華」という漢字を簡易化したもので、（植物の）花の形を模した漢字だよ。

1 カ 🔊 ka

2 いえ 🔊 ie

EN home

Funny Phrases!!

I hate doing chores[1], so I became a karate master[2] and converted my home[3] into a dojo.

家事¹なんて大嫌いだから、空手家²になって家³を道場に改装した。

Writing Styles	家	家	家

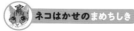 ネコはかせのまめちしき

家 can refer to a house / home or a "master" of some trade.

「家」は職人や達人を表すこともあるよ。

1	カ	🔊 ka
2	うた	🔊 uta
EN	song, sing	

🌸 Funny Phrases!!

What a nice song[1]. And what a splendid singing voice[2]. And, the singer[3] is a parrot!

いい歌[1]だな。なんて素敵な歌声[2]、歌手[3]は…鸚鵡だ！

| Writing Styles | 歌 | 歌 | 歌 |

 ネコはかせの まめちしき

欠 is a person with mouth wide open. It's also found in 飲む (to drink) and 欠伸 (yawn) !

「欠」は、口を大きく開けた人を表すよ。ほかにも「飲む」や「欠伸」にも使われているね。

1 カイ 🔊 kai

2 まわ・る 🔊 mawa・ru

EN rotate, revolve

Funny Phrases!!

Revolving sushi¹ is amazing! There's so much sushi going 'round², I'm dizzy³!

回転寿司¹ はすごいね！目が回る³ ほど寿司が回っている² ！

| Writing Styles |  |

ネコはかせのまめちしき

To "have your eyes spin"（目が回る）is a saying that means you are dizzy.

「目が回る」というのは、「めまいがする」という意味だよ。

1	カイ	🔊 kai
2	あ・う	🔊 a・u
EN	meeting, group	

Funny Phrases!!

In the event hall[1] for the Kitty Lovers' Conference[2], I met[3] a spy from the Puppy Lovers' Association[4].

「にゃんこ同好会[2]」の会場[1] で「わんこ同好会[4]」のスパイに出会った[3]。

| Writing Styles | 会 | 會会 | 会 |

 ネコはかせの まめちしき

Kanji can add nuance to words! 逢う is a pleasant encounter with a friend, while 遭う is to meet with misfortune.

漢字は、言葉にニュアンスを加えることができるんだ！「逢う」は、友だちとのうれしい出会いのときに使うことが多い一方、「遭う」は、不幸に遭遇したときに使うことが多いよ。

| 1 | カイ | 🔊 kai |
| 2 | うみ | 🔊 umi |

EN ocean, sea

Funny Phrases!!

Pirates[1] patrol the ocean[2] and take treasure from the sea bed[3] of the deep sea[4].

海賊[1] は海[2] を巡ったり、深海[4] の海底[3] から宝を持ち去ったりする。

| Writing Styles | 海 | 海 | 海 |

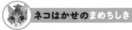ネコはかせの**まめちしき**

海 can refer to oceans, but their names use 洋 (e.g., The Pacific Ocean = 太平洋).

大洋のことも「海」と言うけれど、それぞれの大洋の名前には「洋」を使うよ。(例：太平洋など)

1	ガイ	gai
2	そと	soto
EN	outside, external	

Funny Phrases!!

There's a lot of foreigners[1] **gathered outside**[2] **the ramen shop. Ramen is more popular than I thought**[3]**!**

ラーメン屋の外で外国人が
大勢集まっている。ラーメンは
意外と人気だね！

Writing Styles | お | 外 | 外

ネコはかせの まめちしき

It's common to refer to non-Japanese as 外国
人, but some consider the condensed 外人 to
be rude!

日本ではよく日本人以外のことを「外国人」と言ったりするよ。「外人」と省
略して言うのは無礼だとされているから気をつけよう。

| 1 | ガク | gaku |
| 2 | まな・ぶ | mana・bu |

EN study, learn

Funny Phrases!!

I forgot everything I
learned[1] in school[2]
yesterday. I fail as a
student[3]...

きのう学校[2]で学習[1]したこと
すべて、忘れてしまった。学生[3]
失格…

| Writing Styles | 学 | 学 | 学 |

🐱 ネコはかせのまめちしき

Found in elementary school 小学校, middle
school 中学校, and high school 高等学校.
Students at each level are 小学生, 中学生, 高校
生, respectively.

小学校、中学校、高等学校の学生は、それぞれ小学生、中学生、高校生と言う
よ。

楽

1 ガク、ラク ◀ gaku, raku

2 たの・しい ◀ tano・shī

EN enjoyment, fun, ease

Funny Phrases!!

Ping-pong is so much fun[1]! If I listen to
Queen music[2] before a match, it gets me
psyched up and I score an easy victory[3]!

卓球（たっきゅう）はメチャ楽（たの）しい[1]よ！試合（しあい）の
前（まえ）にクイーンの音楽（おんがく）[2]を聴（き）くと、
気合（きあい）が入（はい）って楽勝（らくしょう）[3]！

| Writing Styles | 乐 | 楽 | 楽 |

 ネコはかせの**まめちしき**

楽 is read "raku" in words related to ease or
fun, and "gaku" when related to music!

「楽（らく）」を「らく」と読（よ）むときは、「容易（ようい）さ」や「おもしろさ」という意味（いみ）に関
係（かんけい）し、「がく」と読（よ）むときは、音楽（おんがく）に関係（かんけい）していることが多（おお）いよ。

| 1 | キ | 🔊 ki |
| 2 | ー | 🔊 ー |

EN spirit, energy

Funny Phrases!!

Everyone **feeling good**¹? What great **weather**² today, right? Let's go hiking in our **favorite**³ spot!

みんな元気¹？きょうはいい天気²ですね！お気に入り³スポットでハイキングしよう！

| **Writing Styles** | 氣 | 氣 | 気 |

ぶせんせいの
ちょっとひとこと

Originally 氣 showing vapor（气）rising off of cooked rice（米）. Simplified to 気.

米を炊くときのゆげを表す（气）＋（米）＝「氣」という漢字が、簡易化されて「気」になったんだ。

帰

1. キ　🔊 ki
2. かえ・る　🔊 kae・ru
EN return home

Funny Phrases!!

It was time to go home[1]. Dz'ibHeb
returned[2] to her home planet,
and I returned to my
home country[3],
America.

もうお帰り[1]の時間だった。デブ
ベブさんは自分の星へ帰還[2]し、
わたしもアメリカへ帰国[3]した。

Writing Styles	帰	歸	帰

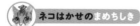

ネコはかせのまめちしき

When returning home, Japanese say ただいま！
and someone in the home responds お帰りなさ
い！

日本では、家に帰ってきたときには「ただいま！」と言うよ。家で待っていた
人は「お帰りなさい！」と返すよ！

37

1	キュウ	🔊 kyū
2	やす・む	🔊 yasu・mu
EN	rest, break	

Funny Phrases!!

Summer vacation[1] I'm very busy.
Everyday, I go running 10 minutes. Then,
I take a break[2] for some ice cream. Then,
a short rest[3].

<ruby>夏<rt>なつ</rt></ruby><ruby>休<rt>やす</rt></ruby>み でも<ruby>忙<rt>いそが</rt></ruby>しいよ。<ruby>毎日<rt>まいにち</rt></ruby>10
<ruby>分<rt>ぷん</rt></ruby>ランニングしてその<ruby>後<rt>あと</rt></ruby>、<ruby>休憩<rt>きゅうけい</rt></ruby>2
してアイスを<ruby>食<rt>た</rt></ruby>べる。そして<ruby>一<rt>ひと</rt></ruby>
<ruby>休<rt>やす</rt></ruby>み 3。

| Writing Styles | 休 | 休 | 休 |

 ネコはかせの**まめちしき**

休 is for physical rest and also for time off or
"vacation" from regular work.

「休」は、<ruby>一時的<rt>いちじてき</rt></ruby>に<ruby>体<rt>からだ</rt></ruby>を<ruby>休<rt>やす</rt></ruby>めるときや、いつもの<ruby>休日<rt>きゅうじつ</rt></ruby>、<ruby>長期休暇<rt>ちょうききゅうか</rt></ruby>にも<ruby>使<rt>つか</rt></ruby>うよ。

1 キョウ 🔊 kyō

2 つよ・い 🔊 tsuyo・i

EN strong

🎵 Funny Phrases!!

When it's time to study¹, strong² coffee is a must!

勉強 するとき、強い² コーヒーは欠かせない！

Writing Styles	強	強	強

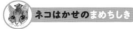 ネコはかせの**まめちしき**

強 can be physically strong, or something that has a powerful effect.

「強」は、身体の強さ、あるいは大きな影響力があることを表すよ。

1 キョウ 🔊 kyō

2 おし・える 🔊 oshi・eru

EN teach

Funny Phrases!!

The church[1] has an English conversation classroom[2]. Jesus Christ himself teaches[3] you English.

教会[1]で英会話教室[2]を開いています。イエスキリスト自身が英語を教えてくれます[3]。

ABC

| Writing Styles | | | |

 ネコはかせのまめちしき

Many churches in Japan offer English classes as part of community outreach.

日本の多くの教会は、奉仕活動として英会話教室を開いているよ。

40

1 ギョク ◀🔊 gyoku

2 たま、
だま ◀🔊 tama,
dama

EN jewel, ball

Funny Phrases!!

Excuse me, there's an eyeball¹ in my fried eggs². Not only that, but the miso soup has a 500 yen coin³ in it!

すみません、玉子焼き²に目玉¹が ある。それだけじゃない、味噌汁 に500円玉³が！

| Writing Styles | | | |

ぶせんせいの
ちょっとひとこと

Three jewels (三) on a string (｜). The extra dot helps tell it apart from king (王).

3つの宝石(三)を1本の糸(｜)でつないでいるよ。残りの点は、「王」という漢字と区別するのに役立つね。

1	キン	🔊 kin
2	かね	🔊 kane
EN	gold, metal, money	

Funny Phrases!!

If you throw the metal disc[1] farther than anyone else, you get the gold medal[2]! And then, you get money[3] as a reward!

金属のディスク[1]を誰よりも遠くに投げると、金メダル[2]獲得！そして褒美にお金[3]がもらえる！

| Writing Styles | 金 | 金 | 金 |

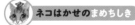 ネコはかせの まめちしき

金 can refer to the planet Venus（金星）and Friday（金曜日）.

「金」は、「金星」や「金曜日」を表すときに使われているんだ。

1	キン	🔊 kin
2	ちか・い	🔊 chika・i
EN	near, close	

🎵 Funny Phrases!!

If you go to the nearby[1] shrine, neighborhood[2] stray cats will approach[3] you looking for food.

近く[1] の神社に行くと、近所[2] の野良猫がエサを求めて近寄[3]ってくる。

| **Writing Styles** | 辵 | 近 | 近 |

🐱 ネコはかせの まめちしき

近 can refer to physical distance and also something that will occur "soon."

「近」は距離のほかに、何かがもうすぐ起こりそうなときにも使うよ。

1 クウ 🔊 kū

2 そら、 🔊 sora,
あ・く a・ku

EN sky, empty, free

Funny Phrases!!

I have free time¹ to take a trip, but the train has no empty seats². Guess I'll just stare blankly into the sky³…

時間が空いて 旅に出たかったけ
ど、電車に空席 はなかった。じゃ、
空 を見てボーっとしようかな…

| Writing Styles | | | |

ぶせんせいの
ちょっとひとこと

A cave opening (穴).（工）lends the sound クウ and the meaning to "penetrate through end to end."

穴と工の組み合わせだね。工は、「クウ」という音と、「端から端まで貫通する」という意味のもとになっているよ。

1	ゲツ	🔊 getsu
2	つき、づき	🔊 tsuki, zuki
EN	moon, month	

Funny Phrases!!

Monday[1] looks to be a crescent moon[2], but the demon summoning requires a full moon[3]. Guess that's a no go.

月曜日 は三日月 のようだが、
悪魔を召喚するには満月 が必
要。ダメか…。

| Writing Styles | 月 | 月 | 月 |

 ネコはかせのまめちしき

See Chapter 2 for a list of months using 月!

Chapter 2 の「月」を使った一覧表を見てみよう！

1 ケン ◀ː ken

2 み・る ◀ː mi・ru

EN see, look, spot

Funny Phrases!!

Look¹ at this! If you stare² at this pattern, a 3D fish becomes visible³. Did you find⁴ it?

これを見て¹！このパターンを見つめる²と3Dの魚が見えてくる³よ。見つけた⁴？

Writing Styles	見	見	見

ぶせんせいの
ちょっとひとこと

The figure of a person with a large eye 目 for emphasis.

大きな目を強調した人の形からできた漢字だよ。

1	ゲン	🔊 gen
2	い・う	🔊 i・u
EN	speech	

Funny Phrases!!

Our languages[1] are different, so I have no idea what they are saying[2]...

言語 が違うため、何を言っている[2] かさっぱりわからない…

Writing Styles	言	言	言

 ネコはかせの まめちしき

言 is found in many kanji related to speech, such as 話 (talk) and 読 (read).

「言」という漢字は、部首として「話」や「読」のように、話すことに関係する漢字に 多くみられるよ。

1	コ	🔊 ko
2	ふる・い	🔊 furu・i
EN	old, ancient	

Funny Phrases!!

I found an old-looking¹ treasure chest in an ancient² labyrinth. Inside was an old³ sword.

古代 の迷宮で古びた 宝箱を見つけた！中に古い 剣があった。

| **Writing Styles** | 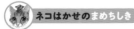 |

ネコはかせのまめちしき

古 doesn't apply to the age of people! In that case, use 老 as in "elderly" 老人 .

「古」は人の年齢には使わないよ！そういうときは、「老人」のように「老」を使おう。

1	ゴ	🔊 go
2	—	🔊 —
EN	noon	

Funny Phrases!!

Sorry, I'm busy today. In the morning[1], I have to settle things with the Beast King, and at noon[2] I need to eliminate the Deep Sea King.

ごめん、きょうは忙しいんだ。午前[1] は百獣の王と決着をつけ、そして正午[2] には深海王の退治があるんだ。

Writing Styles	午	午	午

 ネコはかせのまめちしき

午前 and 午後 are also equivalent to AM and PM, respectively. (e.g.、午前 8 時 = 8 AM)

「午前」と「午後」はそれぞれ、「AM」と「PM」と同じ意味だよ。(例：午前 8 時 = 8AM)

| 1 | ゴ | 🔊 go |
| 2 | あと、 のち | 🔊 ato, nochi |

EN after, later

Funny Phrases!!

The movie starts at 3 PM¹. After that², we're all going to dinner. Alright, see you later³.

映画は午後3時¹ からです。その後² 、みんなで夕飯を食べに行きます。では、後ほど³ 。

| Writing Styles | 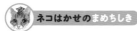 |

ネコはかせの まめちしき

後 is often an unspecified time in the future as in "a later date" 後日 or "in the future" 今後 .

「後」は、「後日」や「今後」のように、不特定の将来の時間のことをよく表すよ。

1	ゴ	🔊 go
2	かた・る	🔊 kata・ru
EN	word, language, tell

🎵 Funny Phrases!!

I love language[1] learning. I can already speak English[2] and French[3]. Next, I want to try Japanese[4]!

語学が大好きだ。もう英語と
フランス語がしゃべれるよ。
次は日本語に挑戦したい！

コンニチワ♪

| **Writing Styles** | 语 | 語 | 語 |

 ネコはかせのまめちしき

Many languages can be expressed as country+
語, such as Russian（ロシア語）or Italian（イタリ
ア語）.

ロシア語、イタリア語のように、多くの言語は、国名＋語で表すよ。

51

1 コウ 🔊 kō

2 くち、ぐち 🔊 kuchi, guchi

EN mouth, opening

Funny Phrases!!

Chaos at the zoo! Escaped bears are making a ruckus! They've blocked the entrance[1], exit[2] and emergency exits[3]! We're all shocked[4]!

動物園は大混乱！脱獄した
熊が暴れている！入口[1] も
出口[2] も非常口[3] も、すべて
熊が塞いでいる！みんな開
いた口[4]が塞がらない！

| Writing Styles | | | |

 ネコはかせのまめちしき

開いた口が塞がらない literally means "unable to shut one's open mouth." It's a state of surprise or shock!

「開いた口が塞がらない」とは、驚きや衝撃を表現するときに使うよ。

1 コウ 🔊 kō

2 — 🔊 —

EN school

〰 **Funny Phrases!!**

There was a call from the school¹. They say giant monsters attacked the school grounds², so there's no school³ today.

学校 から電話があった。校内 に
怪獣が襲ってきたため、きょうは
休校 だそうだ。

Writing Styles	校	校	校

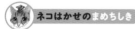

ネコはかせの **まめちしき**

校 is used for primary education, after which students enter "college" and "university" (大学、大学院).

「〜校」というのは、日本では主に初等中等教育を指すよ。その後は主に「大学」「大学院」を使うよ。

| 1 | コウ | 🔈 kō |
| 2 | まじ・わる | 🔈 maji・waru |

EN interact, exchange

Funny Phrases!!

Please turn right at the intersection[1] and stop in front of the International Relations Center[2].

<ruby>次<rt>つぎ</rt></ruby>の<ruby>交差点<rt>こうさてん</rt></ruby>[1] で<ruby>右<rt>みぎ</rt></ruby>に<ruby>曲<rt>ま</rt></ruby>がって、<ruby>国際交流<rt>こくさいこうりゅう</rt></ruby>センター[2] の<ruby>前<rt>まえ</rt></ruby>で<ruby>停<rt>と</rt></ruby>まってください。

| Writing Styles | 亥 | 交 | 交 |

ぶせんせいの
ちょっとひとこと

Originally, the figure of a person crossing their legs.

<ruby>足<rt>あし</rt></ruby>を<ruby>交差<rt>こうさ</rt></ruby>させている<ruby>人<rt>ひと</rt></ruby>の<ruby>姿<rt>すがた</rt></ruby>を<ruby>表<rt>あらわ</rt></ruby>しているよ。

1 コウ　🔊 kō

2 ひかり　🔊 hikari

EN light

Funny Phrases!!

Cats like sunlight[1]. Wolves like moonlight[2]. I like the light[3] of either, but I dislike fluorescent light[4].

猫は日光[1] が好き。狼は
月光[2] が好き。わたしは
どっちの光[3] も好きだけ
ど、蛍光灯[4] がイヤだ。

Writing Styles	光	光	光

ぶせんせいの
ちょっとひとこと

光 is also found in 輝く "to shine".

「光」は、「輝く」という漢字の中にもみられるね。

1 コウ　📢 kō

2 ―　📢 ―

EN craft, construct

Funny Phrases!!

Be careful! This area is under construction[1]. They're adding an AI[2] to the traffic light.

気をつけて！この辺は工事中(こうじちゅう)です。信号(しんごう)に人工知能(じんこうちのう)をインストールしています。

Writing Styles	工	工	工

ぶせんせいのちょっとひとこと

A tool similar to a carpenter's square.

曲尺(かねじゃく)に似(に)た道具(どうぐ)を表(あらわ)しているよ。

1 コウ 🔊 kō

2 たか・い 🔊 taka・i

EN high, tall, expensive

Funny Phrases!!

My giant friend is as tall¹ as a
skyscraper², but his
food bill is expensive³.

巨人の友だちは高層ビル² より背が高い¹。
しかし、食事代も高い¹。

| Writing Styles | | | |

 ネコはかせのまめちしき

Sometimes you may see 高 written as 髙 in a
person's name. It's called "ladder daka" はしご
だか because the middle looks like a tiny
ladder.

ときどき、人の名前で、「高」を「髙」と書くことがあるよ。これは「はしご
だか」と呼ばれているんだ。なぜなら真ん中が小さなはしごのように見えるか
らだよ。

1	コウ、 ギョウ	🔊	kō, gyō
2	い・く	🔊	i・ku
EN	go, do, row, column		

🎵 **Funny Phrases!!**

Let's go eat[1] at the takoyaki place next to the bank[2]. Yikes! What a long line[3]…

銀行[2]の隣のたこ焼きを食べに行こう[1]！うわ！長い行列[3]だ…

Writing Styles	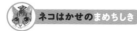

🐱 ネコはかせの まめちしき

Takoyaki (lit. octopus grill) are batter cooked into a ball shape with octopus inside.

「たこ焼き」は、生地の中にたこを入れてボール状に焼いた食べ物だよ！

1 コク　　🔊 koku

2 くに　　🔊 kuni

EN country

Funny Phrases!!

Narita International[1] Airport connects[2] countries all over the world! I've already visited 10 countries[3]!

成田国際 空港は世界中の国々
を繋いでいる！　もう10ヶ国 訪
れたことがある！

Writing Styles	國	国	国

 ネコはかせの まめちしき

国 is a simplification of 國 , which depicts an area 囗 with set borders 口 protected dagger-axe 戈 weilding soliders.

「国」は、「國」を簡単にしたものだよ。領土内（囗）のある地域（口）を武力（戈）で守ることを表しているよ。

1 コン 🔊 kon

2 いま 🔊 ima

EN now, currently

Funny Phrases!!

"Hello¹! Shall we see a movie today²?"
"Hang on a second, I'm checking my schedule now³... Yea,
I'm free all this year⁴.
Let's go!"

「今日は¹！今日²は映画見に行こう？」
「ちょっと待って。今³スケジュールを確認しているよ……はい、今年⁴は暇だ。行こう！」

Writing Styles	こ	今	今

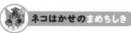 **ネコはかせのまめちしき**

Notice how "Good afternoon! / Hello!" 今日は and "today" 今日は... look exactly the same! These words are often left in hiragana to avoid confusion.

「今日は！」というあいさつと、「今日は…」という文章は、まったく同じ漢字を使っているね！これらは、混乱しないように普通はひらがなを使うよ。

60

1	サ	🔊 sa
2	ひだり	🔊 hidari
EN	left	

Funny Phrases!!

Ah, actually, let's go left¹. Signal a left turn² with your left hand³!

あ、やっぱり左¹に行こう。早く左手³で左折²することを合図して！

| **Writing Styles** | ナ | 左 | 左 |

ぶせんせいの
ちょっとひとこと

A left hand ナ holding a tool エ.

左手（ナ）で道具（エ）を持っている様子を表しているよ。

1 サク ◀︎ᵉ saku

2 つく・る ◀︎ᵉ tsuku・ru

EN make, create

Funny Phrases!!

I intended to make¹ this amazing work²
that the teacher made³, but mine's a
failure⁴…

先生が作った³ すごい作品²を自分で作ろうとした¹ が、失敗作⁴ だ…

| Writing Styles | 作 | 作 | 作 |

ネコはかせの **まめちしき**

The reading for 作 can be tricky sometimes!
Look out for words like "action" 動作 and
"operation" 操作 .

「作」は、「動作」や「操作」のように、ときどき珍しい読み方をするよ。

1	サン、ザン	🔊 san, zan
2	やま	🔊 yama
EN	mountain	

Funny Phrases!!

Mt. Fuji climbing[1] season is from July to September. Both ascending[2] and descending[3] are tough! Don't forget warm clothes!

富士山の山登り[1] シーズンは7月から9月までです。登山[2] も下山[3] も大変ですよ！暖かい服を忘れないでね！

| Writing Styles | | | |

ぶせんせいのちょっとひとこと

Designed after a range of three mountain peaks.

3つの山脈のイメージをもとに作られた漢字だよ。

1	シ	🔊 shi
2	こ	🔊 ko
EN	child	

🏷 Funny Phrases!!

The neighborhood kids[1] won't eat my fried egg & chicken on rice[2], so I gave it to a puppy[3] and kitten[4].

近所の子ども[1] はわたしが作った
親子丼[2] を食べないので、子犬[3] と
子猫[4] にあげた。

| Writing Styles | 子 | 子 | 子 |

🐱 ネコはかせの まめちしき

The 親子 in 親子丼 is literally "parent / child." The rice bowl contains chicken (the parent) and egg (the child)!

「親子丼」の親子は、鶏肉（親）と卵（子）という意味だよ。

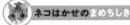

64

止

1 シ 🔊 shi

2 と・まる 🔊 to・maru

EN stop

Funny Phrases!!

No trespassing[1]! You, right there—
please stop[2]!

立入禁止[1]！そこの君、
止まって[2] ください！

| Writing Styles | 止 | 止 | 止 |

 ネコはかせの まめちしき

止まれ or とまれ or トマレ means STOP and is
found on traffic signs or painted on the road.

「止まれ」や「とまれ」、「トマレ」は、交通標識にみられたり、道路の上に書
かれていたりするよ！

| 1 | シ | 🔊 shi |
| 2 | — | 🔊 — |

EN city

🍁 Funny Phrases!!

"I heard there's a ghost in Osaka city[1] that eats takoyaki." "Whaa?? Isn't that just an urban legend[2]?"

「大阪市 には、たこ焼きを食べるお化けがいると聞いた。」「えぇ〜？
それはただの都市伝説 じゃない？」

| Writing Styles | あ | 市 | 市 |

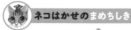 ネコはかせの まめちしき

Takoyaki（たこ焼き）are fried balls of batter with bits of octopus baked in.

たこ焼きは、生地の中にたこを入れて丸く焼いたものだよ。

1 シ 🔊 shi

2 おも・う 🔊 omo·u

EN think

🎵 Funny Phrases!!

"What do you think¹ this is?" "I think² it's better you don't pick that up."

「これは何だと思います¹か？」「拾わないほうがいいと思います²。」

Writing Styles			

 ネコはかせのまめちしき

思（think）is for opinions and conjecture, while 考（think）is for logical thought and rumination.

「思」は単純に意見や推測を表し、「考」は論理的な思考や熟慮を表すよ！

1 ジ 🔊 ji

2 － 🔊 －

EN character, letter

Funny Phrases!!

Kanji[1] study is important! Let's learn one character[2] each day!

漢字 の勉強は大事だよ！毎日1字 学ぼう！

じ・ji

Writing Styles	

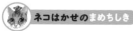 ネコはかせの **まめちしき**

Japanese written phonetically using the alphabet is called ローマ字.

アルファベットを使って日本語を音声学的に書いたものは「ローマ字」と呼ばれるよ。

1 ジ、シ　◀ ji, shi

2 みずか・ら　◀ mizuka・ra

EN self

Funny Phrases!!

It may be scary alone, but if you try and do it yourself[1], you will naturally[2] build confidence[3]!

ひとりは怖いかもしれないが、
自分 でやってみたら、自然 に
自信 がついてくる！

| Writing Styles | | | |

ぶせんせいの
ちょっとひとこと

A picture of a nose. Japanese people point to the nose—not the chest—when referring to one's self.

鼻の形だよ。日本人は、自分のことを話すとき、胸じゃなくて鼻を指さすことがあるよ。

1 シャ　🔊 sha

2 くるま　🔊 kuruma

EN car, vehicle, wheel

Funny Phrases!!

I wonder which is fastest? A car¹, a bicycle² or a train³? Readyyy... GO!

どれが一番速いかな？車 か…自転車 か…それとも電車 か。よ～い スタート！

Writing Styles	车	車	車

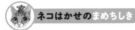 ネコはかせの**まめちしき**

Usually a vehicle, but can also be a wheel as in "pinwheel" (風車).

「車」は大抵は乗り物のことを指すけど、「風車」のように、車輪を表すことも あるよ。

1. シャ、ジャ ◀€ sha, ja
2. やしろ ◀€ yashiro
EN company, shrine

Funny Phrases!!

I quit my company¹ and left society²
behind to work at a shrine³ in the
mountains.

会社¹ をやめて 社会² から
離れて、山の中の 神社³ で
働くことになった。

| Writing Styles | 社 | 社 | 社 |

 ネコはかせの まめちしき

A "shrine" 神社 is of Shinto denomination, while
"temples" お寺 are Buddhist.
神社は神道、お寺は仏教に関係しているよ。

1	ジャク	◀:: jaku
2	よわ・い	◀:: yowa・i
EN	weak	

Funny Phrases!!

Most Japanese train cars are "lightly air-conditioned cars¹." The air conditioner is on, but the effect very weak².

日本の電車は、ほとんどが「弱冷房車¹」です。エアコンはかけていますが、効果はとても弱い²です。

Writing Styles	弱	弱	弱

 ネコはかせの まめちしき

"Survival of the fittest" in Japanese is 弱肉強食. The weak（弱）animal's meat（肉）is the strong（強）animal's meal（食）.

「適者生存」（Survival of the fittest）は、日本語の「弱肉強食」と似ているよ。弱い動物（の肉）は、強い動物の食事になるという意味だ。

1 シュツ　◀≡ shutsu

2 で・る　◀≡ de・ru

EN exit, put out

Funny Phrases!!

We're off[1]! Let's depart[2] on a trip! Huh?
Now, where was the exit[3]?

しゅっぱつ¹ たび で
出発 ！旅に出よう² ！あれ？
でぐち³
出口 はどこだっけ？

| Writing Styles | | | |

ぶせんせいの
ちょっとひとこと

A footprint 屮 exiting from an
opening 凵 .

くぼみ（凵）から足（屮）が出て行く様子を表しているよ。

73

1	ジョ	jo
2	おんな	on'na
EN	woman	

Funny Phrases!!

"Check out my T-shirt! 'Seeking Japanese Girlfriend[1].' Girls[2] are sure to flock in large number!" "Yeah, no, actually they'll run away. You don't understand a woman's mind[3] at all."

「俺のTシャツ見て！〈日本人の彼女募集中〉。面白くて女の子 が大勢集まってくるぜ！」「いや、逆に逃げるよ。まったく女心 がわかってないな…」

| Writing Styles | め 女 女 |

ぶせんせいの ちょっとひとこと

The figure of a woman kneeling with hands crossed.

両手を重ねてひざまずく女の人の様子からできた漢字だ！

1 ショウ 🔈 shō

2 こ、
ちい・さい 🔈 ko,
chī·sai

EN small

Funny Phrases!!

I'll take a small serving[1] of rice, please.
I'm a light eater[2].

ご飯を小盛り[1]にしてください。わたしは小食[2]です。

| **Writing Styles** | | | |

ぶせんせいの
ちょっとひとこと

Small grains scattered on the ground.
小さな穀物が地面に散らばっている様子から作られた漢字だ！

1 ジョウ ◀€ jō

2 うえ、 ◀€ ue,
あ・げる a·geru

EN up, above, over

Funny Phrases!!

"You're quite skilled¹ with chopsticks!"
"Ha ha ha! Watch this. I will use
chopsticks to lift up²
500 kg tuna over³
my head!"

「お箸がお上手 ですね。」
「ははは！ほら見て！お箸で
500キロのマグロを頭の上
に持ち上げる よ。」

| Writing Styles | | 上 | 上 |

ぶせんせいの
ちょっとひとこと

Originally, short line above a long
line. The vertical line is to tell it
apart from the number 2 (二) .

長い横線の上に、短い横線があるね。縦線のおかげで
「二」という漢字と区別できるね。

1 ショク 🔊 shoku

2 た・べる 🔊 ta・beru

EN eat, meal

Funny Phrases!!

I want to make a meal[1]! But there's no ingredients[2]... well, let's eat out[3]!

食事 が作りたい！でも、食材 はない…じゃあ、外食 だ！

| Writing Styles | | | |

 ネコはかせのまめちしき

食 is also found in the kanji 飲 (drink).

「食」という漢字は、部首として「飲」の左側にも入っているね。

1 シン 🔈 shin

2 もり 🔈 mori

EN forest, woods

Funny Phrases!!

A woodland area¹ with so many trees! I wonder if I'll meet a bear here in the woods² ?

なんか木々の多い森林地帯¹！
この森²の中で、熊さんに出会うかしら？

| Writing Styles | 森 | 森 | 森 |

 ネコはかせのまめちしき

3 trees（木）equals woods! In kanji, 3 of something means "many."

3つの「木」は、森に相当するよ。漢字では、3は「たくさん」を意味するんだ。

1 シン　🔊 shin

2 あたら・しい　🔊 a t a r a・shī

EN new

🌸 Funny Phrases!!

There's a new¹ store opening notice in the newspaper² . An outer space travel agency. How cutting edge³…

<ruby>新聞<rt>しんぶん</rt></ruby>² で <ruby>新<rt>あたら</rt></ruby>しい <ruby>店<rt>みせ</rt></ruby>の<ruby>開店宣伝<rt>かいてんせんでん</rt></ruby>！
<ruby>宇宙<rt>うちゅう</rt></ruby>の<ruby>旅行会社<rt>りょこうがいしゃ</rt></ruby>。<ruby>斬新<rt>ざんしん</rt></ruby> だね…

Writing Styles	新	新	新

 ネコはかせの まめちしき

The bullet train 新幹線 is literally the new（新） trunk（幹）line（線）meant to replace the conventional train line（在来線）as the key railway.

<ruby>新幹線<rt>しんかんせん</rt></ruby>とは、<ruby>従来<rt>じゅうらい</rt></ruby>の<ruby>在来線<rt>ざいらいせん</rt></ruby>に<ruby>代<rt>か</rt></ruby>わって、<ruby>新<rt>あたら</rt></ruby>しく、<ruby>主要<rt>しゅよう</rt></ruby>な<ruby>道筋<rt>みちすじ</rt></ruby>（<ruby>幹<rt>かん</rt></ruby>）となる<ruby>鉄道<rt>てつどう</rt></ruby>（<ruby>線<rt>せん</rt></ruby>）という<ruby>意味<rt>いみ</rt></ruby>だよ。

1 ジン、ニン ◀€ jin, nin

2 ひと ◀€ hito

EN person

🏷 Funny Phrases!!

Japanese people¹ have a saying,"10 people² 10 colors." It means people³ all have their different opinions and tastes.

日本人¹ は「十人² 十色」という
言い回しを使う。人³ はそれぞれ
自分の意見や好みがあるという
意味。

| Writing Styles | 人 | 人 | 人 |

🐱 ネコはかせの まめちしき

In English, 十人十色 is similar to "different strokes for different folks."

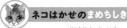

英語には、「異なる人々には異なる褒め方がある」という、「十人十色」と似た
言い回しがあるよ。

1 スイ 🔊 sui

2 みず 🔊 mizu

EN water

Funny Phrases!!

The aquarium¹ takes a day off every Wednesday², and the dolphins come out of the water³ to drink seltzer⁴ and sunbathe.

すいぞくかん1 まいしゅうすいようび 2 ていきゅうび
水族館 は毎週水曜日 が定休日で、
みず3 で たんさんすい4 の
イルカは水 から出て炭酸水 を飲
にっこうよく
んだり日光浴したりする。

Writing Styles	氶	水	水

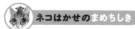 ネコはかせの まめちしき

This also became the water radical （氵）found in kanji like swim （泳ぐ）and ocean （海）.

みず へん なっ かたち およ うみ かんじ つか
水が偏になったときの形 （氵）は、「泳ぐ」や「海」のような漢字に使われて
いるよ。

1 セイ ◀┊ sē

2 ただ・しい ◀┊ tada・shī

EN correct, proper

Funny Phrases!!

What is the correct¹ spelling for
"Japan?" The correct answer² is... A!

Japanのスペル、正しい¹のはどれ？正解²は…Aだ！

 Ⓐ JAPAN

 Ⓑ GIAPON

 Ⓒ JUPUN

Writing Styles	正	正	正

 ネコはかせの **まめちしき**

In Japan, 正 is used to tally numbers like this: 1
一, 2 丅, 3 下, 4 疋, 5 正.

日本では、「正」という漢字は、一（1）、丅（2）、下（3）、疋（4）、正（5）
のように、数を数えるときにも使うよ。

1 セイ 🔊 sē

2 なま、
は・える 🔊 nama,
ha・eru

EN life, birth, raw

Funny Phrases!!

I received a draft beer[1] from the teacher[2]
who grew[3] a beard.

髭を生やした 先生 から生ビール をもらった。

Writing Styles | 生 | 生 | 生

ぶせんせいの
ちょっとひとこと

The shape of 生 was originally a
plant sprouting from the ground.

「生」は、土から植物が生える様子からできた漢字だ！

1	セイ	🔊 sē
2	あお	🔊 ao
EN	blue	

Funny Phrases!!

The young man[1] starting at the blue sky[2] doesn't notice the green traffic light[3].

青空 をボーっと見ている青年 、青信号 に気づいていない。

| Writing Styles | 青 | 青 | 青 |

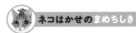

青 is the color blue, but can also mean "green" for traffic lights, plants and vegetables.

「青」は青色のことだけど、信号や植物、野菜など、「緑」のものを表すことも あるよ。

1	セキ	🔊 seki
2	いし	🔊 ishi
EN	rock	

Funny Phrases!!

Hey! Rocks are not to be thrown at people!

コラ！石は人に向けて投げるものじゃない！

| **Writing Styles** | 石 | 石 | 石 |

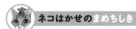 ネコはかせのまめちしき

Be careful not to mix up with "right" 右！ Practicing stroke order can help you learn to differentiate similar-looking kanji.

「右」という漢字と間違えないように！書き順の練習は、似ている漢字の違いを覚えるのに役立つよ。

1 セキ 🔊 seki

2 あか・い 🔊 aka・i

EN red

Funny Phrases!!

I received a love letter with a red[1] heart on it from a total stranger[2] . My face is completely red[3]!

赤の他人[2] から赤い[1] ハートマークのついたラブレターをもらった。顔は真っ赤[3] ！

| Writing Styles | 赤 | 赤 | 赤 |

ぶせんせいの
ちょっとひとこと

Combination of large (大→土) and fire (灬) .

「大」という字が変形して（土）になり、炎（灬）と組み合わさり、「赤」という漢字ができたよ。

1	セン	🔊 sen
2	さき	🔊 saki
EN	previous	

Funny Phrases!!

I heard if the teacher¹ is 15 minutes late to class, you can go home. So, if you'll excuse me²…

先生が授業に15分遅れた場合は、学生は帰っていいと聞いた。それじゃ、お先に失礼 …

| **Writing Styles** | 先 | 先 | 先 |

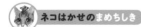
ネコはかせの **まめちしき**

お先に失礼します is a common phrase to excuse yourself when leaving.

「お先に失礼します」は、その場から立ち去りたいときによく使うフレーズだよ。

1	セン	🔊 sen
2	かわ	🔊 kawa
EN	river	

🌸 Funny Phrases!!

There are many rivers¹ in Japan. Riverbanks² are a popular spot for BBQs.

日本には河川¹が多いです。川辺²は
BBQスポットとして大人気です。

| Writing Styles | 丷 | 川 | 川 |

🐱 ネコはかせの まめちしき

川 is found in family names, such as Ogawa (小川), Hasegawa (長谷川) or even Kawabe (川辺)！

「川」は、「小川」、「長谷川」「川辺」のように日本人の名字によくみられるよ。

1 ソウ 🔊 sō

2 はや・い 🔊 haya・i

EN early

Funny Phrases!!

Sold out... I should have come earlier[1].
After all, the early bird[2] gets the worm.

完売か…もっと早め[1]に来れば
よかった。やっぱり、早起き[2]
は三文の徳。

はじめての
かんじ

SOLD OUT

Writing Styles	早	早	早

 ネコはかせのまめちしき

The Japanese saying is literally,"One who rises
early gets 3 coins." Better than a worm, I say!

「早起きは三文の徳」の直訳は、「早起きすると100円くらい得をする」だよ。
虫よりステキだと思う！
※英語を直訳すると、「早起きの鳥は虫（エサ）を捕まえる」となります。

1 ソウ 🔊 sō

2 くさ 🔊 kusa

EN grass

Funny Phrases!!

Once a month, everyone at the apartment does weeding together.

毎月1回アパートのみんなが一緒に草とりをする。

Writing Styles	芓	草	草

ぶせんせいの
ちょっとひとこと

(艹) is two sprouts of grass and appears in many plant kanji, such as flower（花）and leaf（葉）.

(艹) は、「花」や「葉」のように、植物に関係する多くの漢字に使われているよ。

1 ソウ　🔊 sō

2 はし・る　🔊 hashi・ru

EN run

Funny Phrases!!

The race[1] is to that building. Aaaand, run[2] !! ... Hey! You're going the wrong way[3]!

競走_{きょうそう} はあのビルまでだ。さぁ、走_{はし}れ[2] ！！　…おい！逆走_{ぎゃくそう}している[3]よ！

| Writing Styles | 走 | 走 | 走 |

ネコはかせの まめちしき

逆走 also applies to cars driving in the wrong direction.

「逆走_{ぎゃくそう}」は、決_きめられた走行方向_{そうこうほうこう}と反対_{はんたい}の方向_{ほうこう}に走_{はし}っている車_{くるま}にも使_{つか}えるよ。

1 ソク　🔊 soku

2 あし　🔊 ashi

EN foot, leg

Funny Phrases!!

My brother's legs are long[1]. My sister's quick on her feet[2]. I can't hold a candle[3] to either of them.

兄は足が長い[1]。妹は足が早い[2]。わたしは、ふたりの足元にも及ばない[3]。

Writing Styles			

ぶせんせいの
ちょっとひとこと

A picture of the knee joint (□) and foot (止).

膝 (□) から下の足の形 (止) を表しているよ。

1 ソン 🔊 son

2 むら 🔊 mura

EN village

Funny Phrases!!

The mayor[1] of the small village[2] harbors ambitions of world domination.

小さな村の村長は世界制覇の野望を抱いている。

| Writing Styles | お | 村 | 村 |

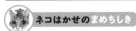 ネコはかせの**まめちしき**

村 is also used for the location of a small, intimate gathering.

「村」は、小さく親密な集まりの場にも使われるよ。

1 ダイ 🔊 dai

2 おお・きい 🔊 ō·kī

EN big

Funny Phrases!!

I'll take a large serving[1] of rice, please. I love[2] rice!

ご飯を大盛り[1]にしてください。お米が大好き[2]です！

| Writing Styles | | | |

ぶせんせいの
ちょっとひとこと

A person standing with arms and legs outstretched.

人が腕と足を広げて立っている様子だよ！

94

1 ダン ◀ dan

2 おとこ ◀ otoko

EN man

Funny Phrases!!

Whether small man[1] or large man[2] , a man[3]'s manliness[4] comes from gentlemanly actions.

小男[1]でも大男[2]でも、男性[3]の
男らしさ[4]は紳士的な行為によ
るもの。

| Writing Styles | 男 | 男 | 男 |

ぶせんせいの
ちょっとひとこと

A combination of rice field 田 and a farming tool 力 .
田んぼと農具の形を組み合わせた漢字だよ。

1	チク	🔊 chiku
2	たけ	🔊 take
EN	bamboo	

Funny Phrases!!

Kyoto has the most beautiful bamboo forests in the world.

京都には世界一美しい竹林がある。

| Writing Styles | 竹 | 竹 | 竹 |

ぶせんせいの ちょっとひとこと

Two stalks of bamboo with leaves hanging off either side.

2本の竹の茎と、垂れ下がっている葉を表しているよ。

1 チュウ 🔈 chū

2 なか 🔈 naka

EN center

🗨 Funny Phrases!!

Pull back the arrow with your middle finger[1] and aim for the direct center[2] of the target. A direct hit[3]!

中指^{なかゆび} で矢^やを引^ひっ張^ばって、的^{まと}の真^まん中^{なか}
を狙^{ねら}え。命中^{めいちゅう} だ！

Writing Styles			

ぶせんせいの
ちょっとひとこと

A large banner in the center of a military unit.

軍隊^{ぐんたい}の中央^{ちゅうおう}にある大^{おお}きな旗^{はた}を表^{あらわ}しているよ。

1	チュウ	🔊 chū
2	むし	🔊 mushi
EN	insect	

🎵 **Funny Phrases!!**

It's not a harmful pest¹, it's a ladybug²!
Let's put away the insecticide³.

害虫 じゃなくてかわいいてんとう虫 だ！じゃ、殺虫剤 はしまって
おこう。

Writing Styles	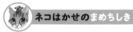

ネコはかせの **まめちしき**

虫 is found mostly in kanji for insects, but also
snake（蛇）and rainbow（虹）！

「虫」という漢字は、昆虫に関係する多くの漢字にみられるだけじゃなくて、
「蛇」や「虹」にも使われているんだ！

1	チョウ	🔊 chō
2	まち	🔊 machi
EN	town	

Funny Phrases!!

The mayor¹ of the small town² hopes for world peace.

小さな町の町長は、世界平和を望んでいる。

| Writing Styles | 町 | 町 | 町 |

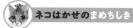 ネコはかせのまめちしき

Towns can be read（name+chō）as in Hamamatsu-chō（浜松町）or（name + machi）as in Hinode-machi（日の出町）.

町の名前は、浜松町や日の出町のように、「～ちょう」や「～まち」と読むよ。

1 デン　◀ den

2 た、だ　◀ ta, da

EN rice field

Funny Phrases!!

Matsuda[1]-san and Tamura[2] -san are playing in the middle of the rice field[3].

松田 さんと田村 さんが田んぼ の中で遊んでいる。

Writing Styles	田	田	田

 ネコはかせの まめちしき

田 is found in many surnames, such as Tanaka (田中), Yoshida (吉田) and Yamada (山田).

「田」 は、「田中」、「吉田」、「山田」 のように、たくさんの名字にみられるよ。

1 デン ◀≡ den

2 — ◀≡ —

EN electricity

🍃 **Funny Phrases!!**

A sudden blackout¹! I telephone² the electric company³ to question them and am told, "You haven't paid your electric bill⁴!"

急に停電¹した！電力会社に電話²して問い詰めると、「お前は電気代⁴を払っていないぞ！」と言われた。

Writing Styles			

 ネコはかせの まめちしき

電車 refers to most local trains, while the bullet train is the Shinkansen（新幹線）.

「電車」は大抵普通列車のことだよ。弾丸列車は「新幹線」と呼ばれてるよ。

| **1** ド | 🔊 do |
| **2** つち | 🔊 tsuchi |

EN earth, ground

Funny Phrases!!

Shoes are forbidden¹ in the sumo ring² ,
but I heard slippers are OK.

土俵 は土足厳禁 ですが、スリッパは大丈夫だそうです。

| **Writing Styles** |  |

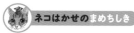 ネコはかせの まめちしき

土 can refer to the planet Saturn（土星）or
Saturday（土曜日）.

「土」は、「土星」や「土曜日」のようにも使えるよ。

1 ドク	🔊 doku
2 よ・む	🔊 yo・mu
EN read	

Funny Phrases!!

I love reading books¹! I want to read²
this book I found in a cave, but it is
indecipherable³.

読書 が大好き！洞窟で見つけた
本を読みたい が、解読不可能 。

| **Writing Styles** | 読 | 読 | 読 |

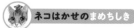 ネコはかせの まめちしき

音（sound）＋ 読（read）is to "read aloud" 音読す
る .

「音読する」というのは、「音」＋「読む」で、声に出して読むという意味だね。

1 ニチ		nichi
2 ひ		hi
EN sun		

Funny Phrases!!

On Sunday[1], I go back to my home country. The days[2] I spent in Japan were fantastic. Thank you, everyone.

日曜日[1] に帰国する。日本で過ごした日々[2] は素晴らしかった。みなさん、ありがとう。

Writing Styles	日	日	日

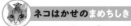 ネコはかせのまめちしき

Sunrise is 日の出 and sunset is 日の入り.

朝、日が出ることを「日の出」、夕方、日が沈むことを「日の入り」と言うよ。

1 ニュウ 🔊 nyū

2 い・る、 🔊 i・ru,
はい・る hai・ru

EN enter, inside

Funny Phrases!!

Doughnuts with jam inside¹ are 10 yen off! Let's enter² the store!

ジャム入り¹のドーナツは10円割引！お店に入りましょう²！

Writing Styles	

ネコはかせの**まめちしき**

Be careful not to confuse with person（人）！

「人」という漢字と間違えないように！

1 ネン 🔊 nen

2 とし 🔊 toshi

EN year

Funny Phrases!!

We had many customers the year before last and last year¹, so from this year we will be open 365 days a year² !

おととしと去年¹はお客様が多かったため、ことしは年中無休²にします！

| Writing Styles |  |

ネコはかせの まめちしき

Calendar years use 年, (e.g., 1982 年 or 2004 年), while ages use 才 or 歳, (e.g., 12 才, 37 歳).

「年」は暦に使うよ。（例：1982年、2004年など）。年齢を表すときは、才か歳を使うよ。（例：12才、37歳など）。

1 ハク 🔊 haku

2 しろ・い 🔊 shiro・i

EN white

Funny Phrases!!

I confessed my feelings[1] for the girl I like in the falling white snow[2].

白い雪が降る中、好きな子に告白した。

| Writing Styles | 白 | 白 | 白 |

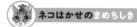
ネコはかせのまめちしき

告白 is "confession" but often used for making known one's romantic feelings.

「告白」は、恋愛感情を表現するときによく使われるよ。

| **1** ブン | 🔊 bun |
| **2** ふみ | 🔊 fumi |

EN literature, culture

Funny Phrases!!

I recite sentences[1] from classical literature[2] to immerse myself in Japanese culture[3].

古文 の文章 を朗読して
日本の文化 に浸る。

| **Writing Styles** | | | |

ぶせんせいの
ちょっとひとこと

The figure of a person with a pattern tattooed on their chest.

胸に刺青が描かれた人を表すと言われているよ。

108

1	ホ、ポ	ho, po
2	ある・く	aru・ku
EN	walk	

Funny Phrases!!

I take my dog for a walk[1] in the park everyday, but she's so energetic, I don't walk[2] as much as I run!

毎日公園で犬の散歩をします[1] が、元気すぎて歩く[2] より走ることになります！

| Writing Styles | 歩 | 歩 | 歩 |

ぶせんせいの
ちょっとひとこと

Simplified over time, this kanji looks like stop 止 and few 少 , but it originally depicted two footrpints-- one in front of the other!

この漢字は、（止）と（少）を組み合わせたものに見えるけど、もともとは縦に並んだ2つの足跡を表しているんだ。

1	ホン、 ポン	hon, pon
2	もと	moto
EN	book, origin	

Funny Phrases!!

I sneakily ate 10 bananas¹ in the bookstore² .

本屋² でバナナを10本¹ こっそりと食べた。

| Writing Styles | 本 | 本 | 本 |

ネコはかせの まめちしき

本 is used to count round, cylindrical objects.

「本」は、柱状のものを数えるときにも使うよ。

名

1 メイ、 🔊 mē,
ミョウ　　myō

2 な　🔊 na

EN name

🎵 **Funny Phrases!!** 🎵

"What's your name¹?" "I'm James. My last name² is Bond. My LINE username³ is SuperSpy007."

「お名前¹ は?」「ジェームズ。名字² はボンド。ラインのユーザー名³ はSuperSpy007。」

Writing Styles | 名 | 名 | 名

 ネコはかせの**まめちしき**

名前 means "name", but when speaking of another person's name, it's polite to add お（お名前）。

ほかの人の名前について話すときは、名前の前に「お」をつけて、丁寧に「お名前」と言うことがあるよ。

1	モク	🔊 moku
2	き	🔊 ki
EN	tree	

Funny Phrases!!

Even monkeys fall from trees. (Japanese proverb meaning "Nobody's perfect").

猿も木から落ちる。

| Writing Styles | 朩 | 木 | 木 |

ネコはかせの まめちしき

木 can refer to the planet Jupiter（木星）or Thursday（木曜日）.

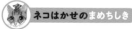

「木」は、「木星」や「木曜日」のようにも使えるよ。

1 ヨウ ◀∃ yō

2 — ◀ミ —

EN ocean, Western

Funny Phrases!!

"The Atlantic Ocean¹ starts with 「大」, but the Pacific Ocean² starts with 「太」."

"Teacher! I need to poo! Is there a Western-style toilet³ here?"

「大西洋¹は「大きい」で始まるが太平洋²は「太い」で始まる。」「先生！ウンチしたい。洋式トイレ³はある？」

| Writing Styles | 洋 | 洋 | 洋 |

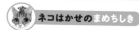 ネコはかせのまめちしき

Japanese-style toilets are notoriously difficult to use for foreigners! Luckily, Western-style are very common nowadays!

和式トイレは、外国人には使いづらくて有名だよ！運の良いことに、最近は洋式トイレが一般的になってきたから大丈夫！

1	リツ	🔊 ritsu
2	た・つ	🔊 ta・tsu
EN	stand

Funny Phrases!!

The private¹ detective standing² in front of the public³ middle school looks super suspicious…

こうりつ³ちゅうがっこう
公立 中学校の前に立っている²
し りつ¹たんてい
私立 探偵はよっぽど怪しそうに
み
見える…

| Writing Styles | 立 | 立 | 立 |

ぷせんせいの
ちょっとひとこと

The figure of a person standing upon flat ground.

たい ら ち めん うえ ひと た よう す つく かん じ
平らな地面の上に人が立っている様子から作られた漢字
だ。

力

1. リョク、リキ ◀ ryoku, riki
2. ちから ◀ chikara
EN power

Funny Phrases!!

I was overwhelmed by the amazing power[1] of the sumo wrestler[2] 's arm strength[3].

力士[2] の腕力[3]、そのすごい力[1] に圧倒されました。

| Writing Styles | 力 | 力 | 力 |

ぶせんせいの ちょっとひとこと

A farming tool similar to a shovel.
耕作に使う農具の形だ。

1	リン	rin
2	はやし	hayashi
EN	forest	

Funny Phrases!!

In the thicket¹ in the bamboo forest² in the woods³... I am completely lost.

森林³ の中の竹林² の中の雑木林¹ の中で…完全に迷子だ。

| Writing Styles | | | |

ぶせんせいの ちょっとひとこと

Two trees（木）to mean dense rows of trees.

2本の木は、密集した並木を表しているよ。

116

1	ワ	🔊 wa
2	はな・す	🔊 hana・su
EN	talk	

Funny Phrases!!

Who are they talking[1] to, I wonder? The phone[2] line is cut.

誰と話している[1]のかしら？
電話[2]の線が切れてるよ。

Writing Styles	話	話	話

 ネコはかせのまめちしき

言（speech）is used to rely information another person said, while 話（talk）is for more involved stories and conversations.

「言」は人が言った情報に対して使うことが多い一方で、「話」は会話など、より話の内容に関連して使うよ！

Can you guess what these sports are?
何のスポーツかわかるかな?

SPORTS KANJI

Q1 **庭球** Hint! Garden 庭 + ball 球

Q2 **野球** Hint! Field 野 + ball 球

Q3 **排球** Hint! Repel 排 + ball 球

Q4 **籠球** Hint! Basket 籠 + ball 球 (Hmm...)

Q5 **鎧球** Hint! Armor 鎧 + ball 球

Q6 **氷球** Hint! Ice 氷 + ball 球

Q7 **避球** Hint! Evade 避 + ball 球

Q8 **蹴球** Hint! Kick 蹴 + ball 球

Q9 **卓球** Hint! Table 卓 + ball 球

Q10 **撞球** Hint! Poke 撞 + ball 球

Answers

1. ていきゅう（テニス）Tennis　2. やきゅう Baseball　3. はいきゅう（バレーボール）Volleyball　4. ろうきゅう（バスケットボール）Basketball　5. がいきゅう（アメフト）American Football　6. ひょうきゅう（ホッケー）Ice hockey　7. ひきゅう（ドッジボール）Dodgeball　8. しゅうきゅう（サッカー）Soccer　9. たっきゅう Table tennis / Ping pong　10. どうきゅう（ビリヤード）Billiards

Chapter 2

List of kanji by concept

種類別の
漢字一覧表

Body 体
<small>からだ</small>

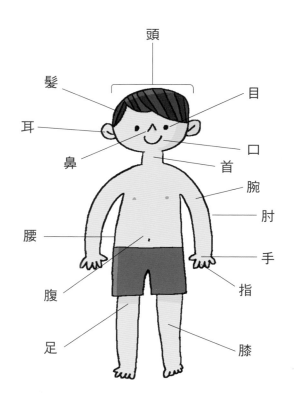

頭

髪

耳

鼻

目

口

首

腕

肘

腰

手

指

腹

足

膝

頭

あたま atama EN head

頭上注意（ずじょうちゅうい） Watch your head!

目

め me EN eye

目蓋（まぶた） eyelid

髪

かみ kami EN hair

散髪（さんぱつ） haircut

鼻

はな hana EN nose

鼻（はな）をかむ to blow your nose

口

くち kuchi EN mouth

口笛（くちぶえ） whistle (using mouth)

耳

みみ mimi EN ear

耳（みみ）たぶ earlobe

首

くび kubi EN neck

首輪（くびわ） collar, necklace

| 腕 | 💬 うで 🔈 ude EN arm |
| | 💡 腕力（わんりょく） arm strength |

| 手 | 💬 て 🔈 te EN hand |
| | 💡 拍手（はくしゅ） applause |

| 足 | 💬 あし 🔈 ashi EN foot |
| | 💡 足元注意（あしもとちゅうい） Watch your step! |

| 膝 | 💬 ひざ 🔈 hiza EN knee, lap |
| | 💡 膝掛け（ひざかけ） lap robe |

| 腰 | 💬 こし 🔈 koshi EN lower back, hip |
| | 💡 腰痛（ようつう） back pain |

| 肘 | 💬 ひじ 🔈 hiji EN elbow |
| | 💡 肘掛（ひじかけ） arm rest |

| 指 | 💬 ゆび 🔈 yubi EN finger |
| | 💡 指を鳴らす（ゆびをならす） to snap your fingers |

💬 はら　📢 hara　EN stomach

💡 腹減った!　I'm hungry!

 　　💬 かた　📢 kata　EN shoulder

💡 路肩　shoulder (of road)

Notice that many body parts kanji include 月! This isn't moon, however, this 月 derives from the kanji for flesh / meat 肉!

体に関する漢字の多くに部首として「月」が含まれているね。でもこれは「月」のことじゃなくて、「肉」という漢字の形に由来するんだ!

Animals 動物
<small>どう ぶつ</small>

蜻蛉

象

熊

虎

鹿

馬

牛

羊

猿

犬

猫

魚

犬	💬 いぬ 🔊 inu
	EN dog

猫	💬 ねこ 🔊 neko
	EN cat

虫	💬 むし 🔊 mushi
	EN insect

魚	💬 さかな 🔊 sakana
	EN fish

鳥	💬 とり 🔊 tori
	EN bird

羊	💬 ひつじ 🔊 hitsuji
	EN sheep

牛	💬 うし 🔊 ushi
	EN cattle

| 猿 | さる saru |
| | EN monkey |

| 熊 | くま kuma |
| | EN bear |

| 蛇 | へび hebi |
| | EN snake |

| 鹿 | しか shika |
| | EN deer |

| 馬 | うま uma |
| | EN horse |

| 虎 | とら tora |
| | EN tiger |

| 象 | ぞう zō |
| | EN elephant |

亀　かめ　kame
EN turtle

兎　うさぎ　usagi
EN rabbit

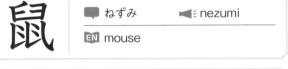

鼠　ねずみ　nezumi
EN mouse

犀　さい　sai
EN rhino

蜻蛉　とんぼ　tonbo
EN dragonfly

土竜　もぐら　mogura
EN mole ("earth"土+"dragon竜")

啄木鳥　きつつき　kitsutsuki
EN woodpecker ("peck"啄+"tree"木+"bird"鳥)

Numbers 数字
すうじ

| 零 | レイ、ゼロ | rē, zero |
| | EN zero | |

| 一 | イチ | ichi |
| | EN one | |

| 二 | ニ | ni |
| | EN two | |

| 三 | サン | san |
| | EN three | |

| 四 | シ、よん | shi, yon |
| | EN four | |

| 五 | ゴ | go |
| | EN five | |

| 六 | ロク | roku |
| | EN six | |

| 七 | シチ、なな  shichi, nana |
| | EN seven |

| 八 | ハチ hachi |
| | EN eight |

| 九 | キュウ、ク kyū, ku |
| | EN nine |

| 十 | ジュウ jū |
| | EN ten |

| 百 | ヒャク hyaku |
| | EN one hundred |

| 千 | セン sen |
| | EN one thousand |

| 万 | マン man |
| | EN ten thousand |

百万	ひゃくまん hyakuman
	EN one million

億	オク oku
	EN one hundred million

兆	チョウ chō
	EN one trillion

京	ケイ kē
	EN ten quadrillion

垓	ガイ gai
	EN one hundred quintillion

秄	ジョ jo
	EN one septillion

穣	ジョウ jō
	EN ten octillion

Months 月 <ruby>月<rt>つき</rt></ruby>

| 一月 | いちがつ　ichigatsu |
| | EN January |

| 二月 | にがつ　nigatsu |
| | EN February |

| 三月 | さんがつ　sangatsu |
| | EN March |

| 四月 | しがつ　shigatsu |
| | EN April |

| 五月 | ごがつ　gogatsu |
| | EN May |

| 六月 | ろくがつ rokugatsu |
| | EN June |

| 七月 | しちがつ shichigatsu |
| | EN July |

| 八月 | はちがつ hachigatsu |
| | EN August |

| 九月 | くがつ kugatsu |
| | EN September |

| 十月 | じゅうがつ jūgatsu |
| | EN October |

十一月	じゅういちがつ
	jūichigatsu
	EN November

十二月	じゅうにがつ
	jūnigatsu
	EN December

Colors 色

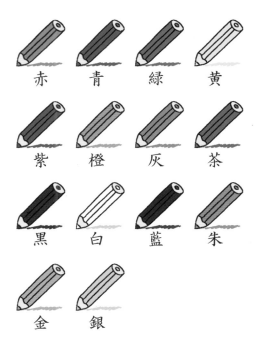

赤　　青　　緑　　黄

紫　　橙　　灰　　茶

黒　　白　　藍　　朱

金　　銀

赤	💬 あか(い) 🔊 aka(i) 🇬🇧 red
青	💬 あお(い) 🔊 ao(i) 🇬🇧 blue
緑	💬 みどり 🔊 midori 🇬🇧 green
黄	💬 き 🔊 ki 🇬🇧 yellow
紫	💬 むらさき 🔊 murasaki 🇬🇧 purple
橙	💬 だいだい 🔊 daidai 🇬🇧 orange
灰	💬 はい 🔊 hai 🇬🇧 grey

| 茶 | 💬 ちゃ　　　🔈 cha |
| | EN brown(color), tea |

| 黒 | 💬 くろ(い)　　🔈 kuro(i) |
| | EN black |

| 白 | 💬 しろ(い)　　🔈 shiro(i) |
| | EN white |

| 藍 | 💬 あい　　　🔈 ai |
| | EN indigo blue |

| 朱 | 💬 しゅ　　　🔈 shu |
| | EN vermilion |

| 金 | 💬 きん　　　🔈 kin |
| | EN gold |

| 銀 | 💬 ぎん　　　🔈 gin |
| | EN silver |

You can add い to a few of these kanji to make adjectives, (e.g., 黒い "black" or 赤い "red.") The kanji for "color" 色 can be added to these and many other words to make colors! (e.g., 朱色 vermilion (colored)" or 桃色 "peach (colored)")

By further adding の and a noun, you can say:

桜色のソックス cherry blossom-colored socks
薔薇色の車 rose-colored car

When describing colors this way, it's common to use flowers and fruits!

「黒い」「赤い」など、いくつかの色の漢字は「い」をつけて形容詞にすることができるよ。また、ものに「色」を足して、様々な色を表すこともできるよ。
「桜色のソックス」「薔薇色の車」のように、「の」をつけて名詞と組み合わせることもできるよ。このような使い方をするときには、色を表現するのに花や果物がよく使われるよ。

Sushi 寿司
すし

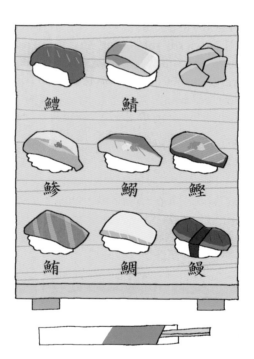

鱧　　鯖

鯵　　鰯　　鰹

鮪　　鯛　　鰻

| 鮭 | 💬 さけ　　　🔊 sake |
| | EN salmon |

| 鮪 | 💬 まぐろ　　🔊 maguro |
| | EN tuna |

| 鯵 | 💬 あじ　　　🔊 aji |
| | EN horse mackerel |

| 鯛 | 💬 たい　　　🔊 tai |
| | EN sea bream |

| 鰹 | 💬 かつお　　🔊 katsuo |
| | EN bonito |

| 鯖 | 💬 さば　　　🔊 saba |
| | EN mackerel |

| 鰯 | 💬 いわし　　🔊 iwashi |
| | EN sardine |

鰻	うなぎ	unagi
	EN eel	

鮎	あゆ	ayu
	EN sweetfish	

鱚	きす	kisu
	EN sand smelt	

鰊	にしん	nishin
	EN pacific herring	

鰈	かれい	karē
	EN righteye flounder	

鮃	ひらめ	hirame
	EN olive flounder	

鰒	ふぐ	fugu
	EN puffer fish	

| 鰤 | ぶり | buri |
| | yellowtail | |

| 鱈 | たら | tara |
| | codfish | |

| 鱧 | はも | hamo |
| | conger eel | |

| 鱸 | すずき | suzuki |
| | sea bass | |

| 𩸽 | ほっけ | hokke |
| | Okhotsk atka mackerel | |

| 鱵 | さより | sayori |
| | Japanese halfbeak | |

| 魬 | はまち | hamachi |
| | adult amberjack | |

Family 家族
かぞく

父

母

お婆さん

お爺さん

姉

弟

| 父 | ちち | chichi |
| | EN father | |

| 母 | はは | haha |
| | EN mother | |

| 兄 | あに | ani |
| | EN older brother | |

| 姉 | あね | ane |
| | EN older sister | |

| 弟 | おとうと | otōto |
| | EN younger brother | |

| 妹 | いもうと | imōto |
| | EN younger sister | |

お爺さん	おじいさん
	ojīsan
	EN grand father

お婆さん	💬 おばあさん
	🔊 obāsan
	🇬🇧 grand mother

| 孫 | 💬 まご　　　🔊 mago |
| | 🇬🇧 grandchild |

The following are usually written in hiragana, but kanji exist if you want to be specific!

以下にあげているものは、通常ひらがなで書くことが多いよ。でも君が漢字に詳しくなりたかったら知っておくと、お得かも？！

伯父さん	💬 おじ・さん
	🔊 oji・san
	🇬🇧 uncle (older)

叔父さん	💬 おじ・さん
	🔊 oji・san
	🇬🇧 uncle (younger)

伯母さん	💬 おば・さん
	🔊 oba・san
	🇬🇧 aunt (older)

144

叔母さん

- おば・さん
- oba・san
- EN aunt (younger)

Older/younger means older or younger than your parent. To remember which is which, think "older" means a person (イ) has more white (白) hair!

君のご両親より年上の場合は伯父、伯母、年下の場合は叔父、叔母を使うよ！

従兄弟

- いとこ
- itoko
- EN cousin (male)

従姉妹

- いとこ
- itoko
- EN cousin (female)

Notice the kanji for brothers (兄・弟) in male cousin and kanji for sisters (姉・妹) in female cousin.

男性のいとこには「兄弟」、女性のいとこには「姉妹」を使うよ。

Seasons 季節
き　せつ

秋

春

冬

夏

| 春 | 💬 はる　　　🔊 haru |
| | EN spring |

| 夏 | 💬 なつ　　　🔊 natsu |
| | EN summer |

| 秋 | 💬 あき　　　🔊 aki |
| | EN fall, autumn |

| 冬 | 💬 ふゆ　　　🔊 fuyu |
| | EN winter |

| 夏至 | 💬 げし　　　🔊 geshi |
| | EN summer solstice |

| 冬至 | 💬 とうじ　　　🔊 tōji |
| | EN winter solstice |

大晦日	💬 おおみそか
	🔊 ōmisoka
	EN New Year's Eve

梅雨

 つゆ

🔊 tsuyu

EN rainy season

Typically early June to mid-July

主に6月初旬から7月中旬の雨が多い季節を指すよ。

花粉の季節

💬 かふんのきせつ

🔊 kafunnokisetsu

EN allergy season

Strongest from mid-February to late April

主に2月中旬から4月下旬が花粉がひどいよ。

桜前線

💬 さくらぜんせん

🔊 sakurazensen

EN Cherry blossom front

Name for the blossoming of cherry blossom, or sakura (桜), trees. Trees in the south and west areas bloom first, and then it moves east across the country.

桜の開花日をつないだ線のことだよ。だいたい南から北上するように進行するよ。

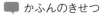

台風

たいふう taifū

EN typhoon

The typhoon "season" begins in June
and lasts until Fall.

台風の季節は、だいたい6月に始まって秋まで続くよ。

年末年始

ねんまつねんし
 nenmatsunenshi

EN year-end holiday break

Literally "year-end, year beginning."
Shorthand for the period of time from
around Christmas until after New
Year's when many people are off work
and busy with holiday activities.

クリスマス前後から新年の休暇が終わるまでを指すよ。多くの人
の仕事が休みで、いろいろなイベントで忙しいよ。

Directions 方位
ほうい

東	■ ひがし　　　◀ higashi	
	EN East	

西	■ にし　　　　◀ nishi	
	EN West	

南	■ みなみ　　　◀ minami	
	EN South	

北	■ きた　　　　◀ kita	
	EN North	

北東	■ ほくとう　　◀ hokutō	
	EN Northeast	

南東	■ なんとう　　◀ nantō	
	EN Southeast	

南西	■ なんせい　　◀ nansē	
	EN Southwest	

北西

- ほくせい
- 🔊 hokusē
- 🇬🇧 EN Northwest

東西南北

- とうざいなんぼく
- 🔊 tōzainanboku
- 🇬🇧 EN North, South East and West

恵方 lucky direction? 恵方って？

On February 3rd, Japanese celebrate 節分 to welcome the coming of Spring. One custom involves eating a large uncut roll of sushi called an 恵方巻 while facing that year's "lucky direction." In 2019, it was East-Northeast.

2月3日は、日本では節分と呼ばれる日で、春の気配が立ち始める日とされているよ。その日は、何事も吉とされるよい方向を向いて、恵方巻と呼ばれる太い巻き寿司を丸かぶりする習慣があるんだ。2019年は、東北東が恵方だったんだ。

Impress your friends with these
challenging kanji!

友だちをびっくりさせよう！

FRUITS KANJI

林檎
■ りんご ◀ ringo **EN** apple

葡萄
■ ぶどう ◀ budō **EN** grapes

檸檬
■ れもん ◀ remon **EN** lemon

鳳梨
■ ぱいなっぷる ◀ painappuru **EN** pineapple

鰐梨
■ あぼかど ◀ abokado **EN** avocado

(Pear 梨 -shaped fruit with crocodile 鰐 -like skin)

These complicated kanji are a real workout!

難しい漢字の練習だ!

 KANJI WITH MANY STROKES

憂鬱

💬 ゆううつ 🔈 yūutsu 🇬🇧 depression

魑魅魍魎

💬 ちみもうりょう 🔈 chimimōryō

🇬🇧 all manner of supernatural creatures

躑躅

💬 つつじ 🔈 tsutsuji 🇬🇧 Rhododendron

躊躇

💬 ちゅうちょ 🔈 chūcho 🇬🇧 hesitation

已己巳己

💬 いこみき 🔈 ikomiki 🇬🇧 similarity

INDEX

●著者紹介

Bret Mayer　ブレット・メイヤー

アメリカ・ニュージャージー州出身。高校生の頃『ドラゴンボール』を
はじめ、漫画やアニメがきっかけで漢字が生き甲斐となる。2012 年
に非漢字文化圏出身者として初めて日本漢字能力検定 1 級に合格。

Born in New Jersey, USA, Bret Mayer was first captivated by
kanji in high school thanks to *Dragonball* among other manga/
anime. In 2012, Mayer became the first westerner to pass
grade 1 of the Japan Kanji Aptitude Test.

カバーデザイン	斉藤　啓（ブッダプロダクションズ）
本文デザイン / DTP	シーツ・デザイン
本文イラスト	イクタケ　マコト / Bret Mayer
筆文字	竹内　一
ダウンロード音声制作	一般財団法人　英語教育協議会（ELEC）
ナレーション	水月優希

本書へのご意見・ご感想は下記 URL までお寄せください。
https://www.jresearch.co.jp/contact/

はじめてのかんじ（漢字）
Let's Explore KANJI

令和元年（2019 年）9 月 10 日　初版第 1 刷発行

著　者	Bret Mayer
発行人	福田富与
発行所	有限会社　Jリサーチ出版
	〒166-0002 東京都杉並区高円寺北2-29-14-705
	電話03(6808)8801(代)　FAX 03(5364)5310
編集部	03(6808)8806
	http://www.jresearch.co.jp
印刷所	(株)シナノパブリッシングプレス

ISBN978-4-86392-449-9